The Scarlet Letter

Nathaniel Hawthorne

Abridged and adapted by Janice Greene

Illustrated by James McConnell

A PACEMAKER CLASSIC

FEARON/JANUS
Belmont, California

Simon & Schuster Supplementary Education Group

Other Pacemaker Classics

Copyright © 1991 by Fearon/Janus, a division of Simon & Schuster Supplementary Education Group, 500 Harbor Boulevard, Belmont, California 94002. All rights reserved. No part of this book may be reproduced by any means, transmitted, or translated into a machine language without written permission from the publisher.

Library of Congress Catalog Card Number: 90–82223

ISBN 0–8224–9352–7

Printed in the United States of America

10 9 8 7 6

Contents

Introduction

The Custom House

It is strange that I am telling readers about myself. Most of the time, I don't even talk about myself to my friends. But now I will tell readers about the three years I spent working at a Custom House.

The Custom House of Salem, Massachusetts, is a large brick building. Not many people come there now. But in some months of the year, it is a busy place. On some mornings, three ships may arrive. Most often they come from Africa or South America. When a ship arrives, the captain will come to the Custom House even before he has seen his own wife. The owner of the ship will come, too. He will be happy if the ship has brought him goods that he can turn to gold. Or, if it has brought goods he cannot get rid of, he will be sad.

I was born in Salem. My family came from Britain two and a quarter centuries ago. One of my ancestors was a Puritan. He was a ruler of the church. He was very hard on people who did not follow the ways of the Puritans. He was an enemy of the Quakers, and he was cruel to them. They remember him in their stories. His son, too, was a very hard man. If he believed a person to be a witch, he sent that person to die. I feel shame for both these men.

After these two men came the long line of my family. We have always lived in Salem. I do not love the place, but it has always been our home. So, after living in other places, I came back to Salem to work for the government. And, one fine morning, with papers from the President in my pocket, I walked up the stone steps of the Custom House. My job was to be the chief executive officer.

Most of the men who worked at the Custom House had been sea-captains. And most were very old. Two or three of them, I was told, were not very well. They only came to the Custom House during the warm months. Then, when they felt like it, they went back home to bed.

Most of the men working for me were Whigs. If I had cared about politics, since I was a Democrat, I would have gotten rid of them. At first they were afraid of me. But they soon learned they had nothing to worry about.

The Custom House Inspector was old but very strong and fit. He had had three wives and twenty children. He looked like a wonderful man. But he had no deep thoughts, no deep feelings. In fact, he was very much like an animal.

Then there was the Collector, General Miller. He had been a brave soldier. Now he was old, and it was hard for him to come up the steps of the Custom House. For all I know, he had killed many men. But there was nothing mean in his heart. I have never known a man who was kinder than he was.

These were the kinds of men I now spent my time with. My life was very different than before. I had lived at Brook Farm. I had spent much time with Emerson and Thoreau. Now it seemed right to try a new side of myself.

I no longer wanted to have my name on a book. It made me smile to think that now my name was marked on bags of pepper, baskets of dye, and other goods from the ships. But the past was not dead. I had put to rest all thoughts of writing. But they came alive again.

One slow, rainy day, I found something very strange. I was looking into a pile of old papers when I found a small package. In it were papers written by a man named Jonathan Pue. This man had worked at the Custom House long ago. Also inside was a piece of red cloth. It was old and worn. The cloth was decorated with gold thread. It made the shape of a letter—the letter A.

I wondered what the letter meant. I held it to my chest. The reader may smile at this—but I felt as if the letter burned me. I let it drop to the floor.

Then I read a few pages written by Jonathan Pue. They were about a woman named Hester Prynne— and the scarlet letter.

I felt as if Jonathan Pue had met me in the Custom House. I felt as if he asked me to write the story of Hester Prynne. And I said to the ghost of Mr. Pue, "I will!"

I thought quite a lot about the story I wanted to write. But the people I wanted to write about would not come to life. I could not give them real feelings. They seemed like dead people. It seemed they said to me, "Any power you once had to write a story is gone. You have traded it for the little gold you get from the government. Go, then, and earn your pay!"

I think that if I had stayed a long time at the Custom House, the story of "The Scarlet Letter" would have never been written. But after I had been there three years, the Whig candidate, Zachary Taylor, was elected President. I had never been a very strong Democrat. So I thought I had a better chance of keeping my job than the other Democrats. But I was the first one to go!

In the end, I felt everything was for the best. I bought paper, ink, and pens. I opened my desk and became a writer once again.

1 A Woman on the Scaffold

Many men and women stood waiting at the door of the Boston prison. In front of the building, weeds were growing. They were as ugly as the prison itself. But on one side of the entrance was a wild rosebush. Now, in June, it was covered with flowers.

This rosebush is close to the beginning of our story. So we will pick one of its flowers, and give it to the reader. We hope this flower will be a sweet lesson that might be found in our story. Perhaps the rose will make the end of this story less sad.

The people in front of the prison entrance were Puritans. Their faces were not kind.

One hard-faced woman said, "The magistrates are good men. But they have been too kind. They have given Hester Prynne a light sentence. She should have stood before us women! Then her sentence would not be so light!"

Another woman said, "People say that Reverend Dimmesdale is very sad that such a thing happened in his church."

A third woman said, "The magistrates are good men. But they are too kind. That is the truth. They should have put a hot iron on Hester Prynne's head. But she won't care what they put on the front of her dress! She may even cover it up and walk around as if nothing happened!"

A young wife said softly, "Let her cover the mark if she wants to. It will always hurt inside her heart."

"Quiet," a man said. "The prison door is opening. Here comes Hester Prynne."

The door of the prison opened. The town beadle came out. He was wearing his sword. With his right hand placed upon the shoulder of a woman, he led her through the door.

In her arms the woman held a baby. The baby blinked in the bright sunlight. On the woman's dress was a red cloth. It was in the shape of the letter A. The scarlet A was outlined in gold thread.

The woman was young and tall and beautiful. She had rich dark hair and deep black eyes. She looked out at all the men and women. Her face was hot and red. But she had a proud smile.

"Let us go by," said the beadle. "In the King's name, let us go by! And I promise you, every man, woman, and child will have a good look at her. Come, Hester Prynne! Show your scarlet letter in the marketplace!"

The beadle led Hester through the crowd. Her face was quiet. But she may have felt as if her heart were down on the street, where people could walk on it.

The beadle led her into the marketplace and up onto the scaffold. There she stood. She did not make a sound. Below her was the crowd. Behind her was a balcony. On the balcony sat the governor, the ministers, and other important men of the town.

Hester stood silently. A thousand eyes were on her. She felt the weight of those eyes. She thought she would scream or go crazy. Then her mind escaped to the past. She saw herself as a young girl in England. She remembered her home and her parents' faces. She saw the face of an older man. This man had a left shoulder that was higher than his right one.

All at once, she was back on the scaffold. Here were the hard eyes of the crowd. Here was her baby. And here was the scarlet letter on her dress. This was her life now. Everything else was gone!

Hester looked at the crowd. She saw an Indian standing with the people of the town. Next to the Indian was a white man, a stranger. He had one shoulder higher than the other. Hester saw who the man was. Suddenly, she hugged her baby hard—so hard that the poor babe cried.

The stranger saw Hester looking at him. Slowly, he put a finger on his lips. Then he turned to the man next to him. He asked, "I pray you, good sir, who is this woman? Why does she stand in shame before the town?"

"You must be a stranger, or you would know about Hester Prynne," the man replied. "She has done great wrong in Reverend Dimmesdale's church."

"That is true. I am a stranger. I have had great troubles on land and at sea. For a long time I have been a prisoner of the Indians. They have brought me here to ask for my ransom. So I know nothing about this woman and why she stands at the scaffold."

The man said, "That woman was the wife of an Englishman. He had decided to come here to live. He sent his wife over first. But that was two years ago. There has been no word of him. And his young wife was all alone, you see——"

"Aha! I see," said the stranger. "And who is the father of the baby?"

"We still do not know," said the man. "Hester Prynne will not tell us. The magistrates have not been able to guess who he is. But they have been kind to her. The usual sentence for her crime is death. But she is young. And her husband is probably at the bottom of the sea. So her sentence is light. She must stand at the scaffold for only three hours. And she must wear her scarlet letter for the rest of her life."

"A wise sentence!" said the stranger. "But it bothers me that her partner is not standing there with her.

But we will know him!—we will know him!—we will know him!"

The stranger bowed to the other man. He and the Indian walked through the crowd.

While all this happened, Hester watched the stranger. It was awful to stand before the crowd. But she was glad so many people were between herself and the stranger. She did not want to face the stranger alone.

Suddenly a loud voice came from the balcony. It said, "Listen to me, Hester Prynne."

Hester turned white and began to shake. It was John Wilson's voice. He was the oldest pastor in Boston. He said, "I have told Reverend Dimmesdale that you must confess. You must tell us the name of the man you have sinned with. He says it would be wrong. He says we must not make you open your heart in the light of day. Not in front of so many people. But what do you say, Reverend Dimmesdale? Who will deal with this poor woman's soul? You or I?"

Governor Bellingham said, "Good Reverend Dimmesdale, it is up to you to save this woman's soul."

The Reverend Arthur Dimmesdale bent his head. His brown eyes were large and sad. He was young, but people had great respect for him. He had learned many things from his books. And he had a deep love of God.

"Hester Prynne," he said, "I ask you to name your partner. He may not be brave enough to say who he is. But he should stand up here with you. It is better for him to stand in shame than to hide a guilty heart."

His voice was sweet, rich, deep, and broken. Everyone felt moved by his words. Even Hester's poor baby held out her little arms to the pastor. But Hester shook her head.

"Say the man's name!" said Reverend Wilson. "And if you ask us to pardon you, we may take the scarlet letter off your dress."

"Never," said Hester, looking at Reverend Dimmesdale. "The letter is burned too deep inside me. You cannot take it off."

"Speak," said a cold voice from the crowd. "Speak, and give your baby a father!"

Hester knew who said these words. She turned as white as death. "I will not speak!" she said. "My baby must find a Father in heaven. She will never know one on earth!"

"She will not speak," said Mr. Dimmesdale, softly. "How strong and kind a woman's heart is! She will not speak!"

Reverend Wilson began a long sermon on sin. Many times he mentioned Hester's scarlet letter. Hester stood without a sound. The light was gone from her eyes. She could take no more. Her baby screamed and cried. The pastor went on and on. His voice was like thunder. Then at last it was over. She was led back to prison.

2 The Interview

When she went back to prison, Hester began to act as though she were crazy. Master Brackett, the jailer, had to watch her every minute. He was afraid Hester would hurt herself or her poor baby. The baby seemed to feel all of the mother's sadness. The child twisted and cried in pain. Finally, the jailer sent for a doctor.

This doctor was staying at the jail, though he had done no wrong. The prison was the only place for him to stay at the time. He had been a prisoner of the Indians. Now the town officials were arranging for his ransom.

This was the same man Hester had seen in the crowd. The jailer introduced him as Roger Chillingworth. Hester looked up at him. She became as still as death.

"Please, friend," said the doctor to Master Brackett. "Leave us alone. I promise you, your jail will soon be quiet."

"If you can accomplish that, your skill is great," said the jailer. "The woman has seemed to have an evil spirit in her. I was going to drive Satan out of her with a whip."

The doctor went quietly into the room. He looked over the baby carefully. Then he took some medicines from a leather bag. One of these medicines he mixed with water. "Here, woman!" he said. "Give this to your child."

Hester looked at him. "Would you take revenge on a baby?" she whispered.

"Foolish woman!" said the doctor. "Why should I hurt this poor baby?" He took the baby in his arms and gave her the medicine. The baby became quiet. Soon she fell into a deep sleep.

The old man turned again to Hester. "I have learned many new secrets while living with the Indians," he said. "Here is one of them. It will calm you down." He mixed a second medicine and held it out to her.

Hester looked into his face. She wondered what he was doing. "I have thought about death," she told him. "I have even wished to die. Is there death in this cup? If there is, I ask you to think again, before I drink it. See! Even now it is at my lips."

"Drink, then," he said. "Do you know me so little, Hester Prynne? Even if I wanted revenge, how could I do better than to let you live—and wear this burning shame on your dress?"

Hester drank. The doctor took a seat beside her.

"Hester," he said. "I won't ask what happened. I was a fool, and you were weak. I am an old man, always reading my books. You are young and

beautiful. I should have guessed this would happen.
From the moment we were married and walked down
the church steps together, I should have seen the
burning scarlet letter at the end of our path!"

Hester was hurt by his words. She said, "You know
that I was honest with you. I felt no love for you.
And I never pretended to love you."

"True," he said. "I was a fool! But until I met you,
my life seemed empty. I wanted so much to have a
wife and a home. And so I drew you deep into my
heart."

"I have done you great wrong," said Hester.

"We have wronged each other," said the doctor. "But there is a man who has wronged us both. Who is he?"

"Do not ask me!" said Hester. "You will never know!"

The doctor's smile was dark. "Never?" he said. "You may cover up your secret from everyone else, but I will find him. Let him live. I will not hurt him. But he will be mine!"

Hester said, "Your words sound kind. But I am afraid for him!"

The doctor said, "One more thing. You have kept his secret. Now keep mine. Tell not a human soul that I was once your husband. Above all, do not tell your lover. If you tell him, beware! His good name, his position, and his life will be in my hands. Beware!"

"I will keep your secret," said Hester.

"Swear it!" he said.

And so she did.

"And now, Mistress Prynne," said old Roger Chillingworth, "I leave you alone—alone with your baby and the scarlet letter! How is it, Hester? Do you have to wear the letter in your sleep? Are you not afraid of bad dreams?"

"Why do you smile at me like that?" asked Hester. "Are you like the devil that lives in the woods? Have you made me make a promise that will destroy my soul?"

"Not your soul," he said. "No, not yours!"

When Hester's prison sentence was over she found a small, empty house on the edge of town. And there she made her home with her baby girl. Though Hester was an outcast, she had a way to make a living. She had a fine skill at needlework. People paid Hester to decorate scarves, caps, gloves, and collars. But no one ever asked her to decorate a bride's white veil.

Hester made her own clothes in dark colors and of rough cloth. But she dressed her child in rich and strange clothes. These clothes seemed to match the strange charm of the little girl.

When Hester had any extra money, she gave it to the poor. Often, they took her money with harsh words. The women who bought her work also said mean things to her. Hester never talked back to them. But she would never say a prayer for them. For the words of her prayers might have turned into curses.

Hester felt the pain of her scarlet letter everywhere she went. If she went to church, the pastor would often talk about her in his sermon. She became afraid of children. They would follow her, calling her names.

But every now and then, Hester felt she was not the only one who had done wrong. The scarlet letter seemed to give her a strange power to see the sins of other people. She would get a strange feeling as she walked by a certain man or woman. It seemed that these people had secrets inside them. And if those secrets were told, these people might wear scarlet letters like Hester's.

Hester was an outcast. But she was never alone. There was no friend to watch her baby, so the little girl went with her everywhere.

Hester named her baby Pearl. She did so because the little girl had cost her so much and because the child was her only prize. Pearl was a beautiful little girl. She was full of high spirits and very smart. But since the child had been made in sin, Hester was afraid she would turn out badly.

Sometimes Pearl seemed to be under a spell. As she grew older, Hester could not control her. Pearl would get a certain look in her bright, black eyes. That look was very smart, but it was also very strange and sometimes very mean. Hester wondered sometimes if Pearl were really a human child. Then Hester would run to her daughter. She would hug and kiss her, as if to make sure that Pearl was real.

Soon, Pearl became old enough to play with other children. But this could never happen. Like her mother, Pearl was an outcast. People said Pearl was not fit to play with their children. Somehow, Pearl knew this. She watched little Puritan children, but she never tried to play with them. If they came up to her, she became very angry. She would throw stones at them.

One strange thing about the child has not been said. When she was a little baby, there was one thing she seemed to notice before anything else. This was her mother's scarlet letter. Often Pearl would look at the letter with a strange light in her eyes and a strange smile on her mouth. When she did this, it seemed as if an evil spirit were inside her.

One day Pearl made a game of throwing wildflowers at her mother's dress. Whenever she hit the scarlet letter, she would jump up and down.

Hester sat still and looked sadly into Pearl's wild eyes. At last, Hester said, "Pearl, what are you?"

"Oh, I am your little Pearl!" said Pearl.

Hester was very sad. But she spoke almost as if she were being funny. She said, "Then tell me what you are, and tell me who sent you to me."

"Tell me, mother!" said Pearl. All at once she was very serious. She ran to Hester. "Do tell me!" she said.

"Your Father in heaven sent you," said Hester.

Pearl touched the scarlet letter on her mother's dress. She said, "He did not send me. I have no Father in heaven!"

Hester said, "Pearl! You must not talk like that! Our Father in heaven sent us all into the world. Even me."

Pearl was no longer serious. She went dancing around the floor. She laughed as she said, "Tell me! Tell me! It is you who must tell me!"

But Hester could not answer her daughter. For she was not sure herself.

3 A Visit to the Governor

One day, when Pearl was three years old, Hester took her to the home of Governor Bellingham. Hester was bringing a pair of gloves to the governor. She had decorated them with embroidery and fringe. But her real reason for the visit was far more important.

Hester had heard some very bad news. The governor and other leaders of the town were talking about taking Pearl away from her. These people felt that Hester was not a good mother for the little girl.

This day, Hester had dressed Pearl in a strange and beautiful dress. It was deep red, and it was embroidered all over with gold thread. Pearl looked like the scarlet letter come to life.

A servant told Hester the governor was out walking wtih some visitors. Hester and Pearl waited in the governor's great hall. When Pearl saw the rosebushes outside in the garden, she began to cry for a red rose. She would not stop.

"Quiet, child, quiet!" said Hester. "Do not cry, dear little Pearl! I hear voices in the garden. The governor is coming, and other gentlemen are with him."

Governor Bellingham came walking toward the house. Beside him was Mr. Wilson. Walking behind

22

them were the young Reverend Dimmesdale and the doctor, old Roger Chillingworth. Roger Chillingworth was now known as a doctor of great skill. He had become a close friend of Reverend Dimmesdale, who was not well.

The governor was the first one to see Pearl in the hall. He was surprised to see a child in such a rich dress. "What have we here?" he asked.

"My name is Pearl," she answered.

Mr. Wilson whispered to the governor, "This is the child we have been talking about. And there is her mother, Hester Prynne!"

Governor Bellingham turned to Hester. His voice was hard. He said, "Hester Prynne, there has been a lot of talk about you lately. We do not know if it is right for someone like you to bring up a child. Tell us, what can you do for this child?"

Hester touched the letter on her dress. "I can teach my little Pearl what I have learned from this!" said Hester.

"We shall see," said the governor. He turned to Reverend Wilson. "Mr. Wilson, please see if this child has learned what a good Christian should know."

"Pearl, can you tell me who made you?" Mr. Wilson asked.

Now Pearl knew very well who made her. Hester had taught the little girl about the Father in heaven and much more. But Pearl said that she had not been made at all. She said she had been picked by her mother from the wild rosebush that grew by the prison door.

Pearl probably said this because she had seen the red roses in the governor's garden. Also, she had passed the prison rosebush on her way to the governor's house.

Old Roger Chillingworth smiled and whispered something in Reverend Dimmesdale's ear. Hester looked closely at the doctor. Even though she was very worried about Pearl, she saw a change in the old man. He had become ugly. His dark face seemed even darker.

Meanwhile, the governor was shocked at what Pearl had said. "This is awful!" he said. "Here is a child three years old, and she cannot tell who made her! I think we have all the answers we need."

Hester pulled Pearl to her side. She said, "God gave this child! She is what makes me happy! She is my torture, too! Pearl keeps me here in life! Pearl punishes me, too! Can you not see that she is the scarlet letter! You will not take her! I will die first!"

"My poor woman," said Mr. Wilson. "They will take good care of the child—much better than you can do it."

Hester's voice was almost a scream. "I will not give her up!" she said. She turned to Mr. Dimmesdale. "Speak up for me!" she cried. "You were my pastor.

25

You know me better than most men. Speak for me! You know what is in my heart. You know what a mother's rights are. You know how much stronger they are when a mother has only a child and a scarlet letter. Do it! I will not lose the child! Do it!"

The young pastor came up to them. When he felt bad, he held his hand over his heart. He was doing it now. He looked thinner and more tired than on that day when Hester stood on the scaffold. And his large, dark eyes looked sad and hurt.

The pastor's voice shook. It was sweet, but it had much power. He said, "There is truth in what Hester says. The child was given to her by God. God meant to bless Hester. The child is the only blessing in her life! God also meant to punish her. See how Hester even dresses her child like her own scarlet letter!"

"You say it well," said Mr. Wilson.

Reverend Dimmesdale went on, "Every time Hester sees her child, she remembers that she once did great wrong. The child will keep her from falling into sin again. And if Hester can show Pearl the way to heaven, the child will bring her mother with her!"

Old Roger Chillingworth smiled at Mr. Dimmesdale. Chillingworth said, "You speak with strange feeling, my friend."

"And there was much truth in what he said," said Reverend Wilson. "So, what do you say, Master

Bellingham? Has he not said a good word for the poor woman?"

"So he has," said the governor. "As long as the woman does not get into trouble again, we will leave things as they are."

The young pastor stepped back a little. Pearl went up to him. She took his hand and put it on her cheek. How quiet and sweet she was. Hester asked herself, "Is that my Pearl?"

Then the little girl laughed and danced down the hall. Her step was so light that Mr. Wilson wondered out loud if her toes even touched the ground.

"A strange child!" said old Roger Chillingworth. "It is easy to see her mother in her. If we watched her very closely, I wonder if we could guess who her father is."

"No, it would be wrong," said Mr. Wilson. "It is better to pray on it, and leave that question alone. So every good Christian man should be as kind to the poor child as if he were her father."

Hester and Pearl left the house. As they went down the steps, Mistress Hibbins threw open her window. She was the mean sister of the governor. A few years later, she would be put to death as a witch.

"Hist, hist!" said Mistress Hibbins. "Will you go to the forest with us tonight? The devil will be happy to see you."

Hester smiled proudly. "Please tell him I cannot come!" she said. "I must stay at home and be with my little Pearl. If they had taken her away from me, I would have been happy to go with you. And I would have written my name in the devil's book. With my own blood!"

"We will see you there soon," said the witch-lady with a frown.

4 An Evil Doctor

The people of Boston were very happy when Roger Chillingworth became Reverend Dimmesdale's doctor and friend. The young pastor was not well. People were worried about him. They hoped the doctor's great skill could help the young pastor. Some people even said that heaven brought the doctor to Boston. They said heaven had taken the doctor from a university in Germany, lifted him through the air, and set him down in front of Reverend Dimmesdale's house!

After a time, Roger Chillingworth said he could take better care of Mr. Dimmesdale if they lived in the same house. Mr. Dimmesdale's friends arranged for both men to live in the home of a widow who had a good name. The old doctor wanted to give all his skill and learning to help the pastor. But Reverend Dimmesdale gently told him no.

"I need no medicine," he said.

But how could the young pastor say no? Every Sunday his cheeks were paler and thinner. His voice shook. His hand was always on his heart now, as if it hurt him every minute.

Arthur Dimmesdale's body was strongly joined to his soul. He was a very sensitive man, with a great imagination. It seemed to the doctor that any sickness of the reverend's body would have its roots in the mind and heart. So Roger Chillingworth dug into the pastor's mind. He dug slowly and carefully, like a man looking for a treasure in a dark cave.

One day, the young pastor was watching Roger Chillingworth in his laboratory. The old doctor often looked for herbs to make into medicines. Now he was looking at some dark, ugly plants.

The young pastor asked, "Where did you get those herbs with such a dark, flabby leaf?"

"In the graveyard," said the doctor. "They were growing on a grave that had no tombstone or any other marker for the dead man. The weeds were growing from the man's heart. Perhaps they show that a terrible secret had been buried with him. Perhaps it was a secret he should have told while he was alive."

Mr. Dimmesdale said, "Perhaps he wanted to tell, but he could not. But I believe that on the great judgment day, all terrible secrets will be told. And people who tell them will feel free and happy."

Roger Chillingworth looked quietly at the young man. He said, "Then why not tell these secrets here, on earth? Why should people not find the great joy of telling their secrets?"

Mr. Dimmesdale held his chest hard, as if it hurt him. "Some men could do no good on earth if people knew their secrets," he said. "They could not work for God's glory, or for other people."

"Those men lie to themselves," said Roger Chillingworth. "Are you saying that living a lie is better? Better for God's glory? Better for other people? Better than truth? Believe me, those men lie to themselves!"

"You may be right," said the young pastor, as if he didn't care. He was very good at escaping talk that made him feel bad.

As time went by, people began to see a change in Roger Chillingworth. Before, he seemed quiet and thoughtful. Now there was something ugly and evil in his face. People said that the fire in his laboratory came from hell, and his face was getting dark from the smoke.

Some people said that Roger Chillingworth was a worker for the devil, or the devil himself. They said he had come to test Reverend Dimmesdale's faith in God. The townspeople were sad for their reverend. But everyone was sure the devil would lose.

One day Reverend Dimmesdale sat reading in his chair. He fell into a deep, deep sleep. He did not wake when Roger Chillingworth came into the room.

The old doctor walked up to the sleeping Dimmesdale. He pulled open the clothing that covered his chest. The doctor looked hard at the young man's chest. Then he turned away. On the old man's face was a wild look of wonder, joy, and horror! If a man had seen Roger Chillingworth's face at that moment, he would have seen a face like the devil's. For this is what the devil looks like when a soul is lost from heaven and won to hell.

After this, things seemed the same between Mr. Dimmesdale and Roger Chillingworth. But now the old doctor had a plan. In small ways, he made the pastor feel his sin again and again. He made Mr.

Dimmesdale feel afraid all the time. But he did this quietly and carefully. The young man never knew the doctor was his enemy. Mr. Dimmesdale came to hate and fear the old man. But he never knew the reason for his feelings. He thought there was something wrong with him for not liking the doctor. After all, the doctor always spoke to him in such a kind way.

Mr. Dimmesdale was sick. Deep trouble was in his soul. His worst enemy tortured him night and day. At the same time, the people of the town loved him more than ever. His sermons were full of sadness and power. His words seemed to come from heaven. Even the ground he walked on seemed holy.

When Reverend Dimmesdale gave his sermons, he told people he was evil. He said his sins were worse than anyone else's. And people would say to themselves. "Oh, he is a saint!" They never knew the truth of the pastor's words. But Mr. Dimmesdale knew he was being loved for a lie. He hated lies. Most of all, he hated himself.

The young pastor kept a whip locked in a dark closet. He used it to whip himself for his sins. He also went many hours without eating. He kept himself up late at night. His thoughts tortured him. One late night, the pastor thought of something that might bring him some peace.

As if he were in a dream, he left the house. He walked toward the marketplace. He came to the scaffold, where Hester Pyrnne had stood seven years before.

Reverend Dimmesdale climbed up and onto the scaffold. The dark sky was full of clouds. No one could see him. But it seemed to him as if the whole earth and sky were looking at a scarlet letter on his chest. All at once, he heard a laugh, a child's laugh.

"Pearl! Little Pearl!" he said. Then he dropped his voice and called "Hester! Hester Prynne! Are you there?"

"Yes, it is Hester Prynne!"

The pastor heard her steps coming closer from the sidewalk.

"Where have you come from, Hester?" asked the pastor.

"I have been watching at a deathbed," answered Hester. "The former Governor Winthrop has died. I have measured him for a robe and now I am going back home."

Reverend Dimmesdale said, "Come up here, Hester. You and little Pearl. You have both been here before, but I was not with you. Come up here once again, and we will stand together. All three of us!"

Hester did not say a word. She walked up the steps. She held little Pearl by the hand. The minister felt for the child's other hand and took it. At that moment, he felt a rush of new life into his heart. The three of them made an electric chain.

"Reverend!" whispered little Pearl.

"Yes, child?" asked Mr. Dimmesdale.

"Will you stand here with mother and me, tomorrow at noon?" asked Pearl.

"No, my little Pearl," said the pastor. "I will stand with you on the great judgment day, but not tomorrow."

Pearl laughed. All at once, a light shone far and wide over the cloudy sky. The light was made by a meteor, which was burning itself out. The strange light was so strong it made the street as bright as day.

The pastor looked up at the sky. He saw a huge letter—the letter A—made by the red light. There was probably no such shape at all. But this was what his guilty mind saw. At the same time, Mr. Dimmesdale saw that Pearl was pointing her finger at Roger Chillingworth. He was standing close to the scaffold. In the strange light of the meteor, he looked like the devil.

Suddenly, Mr. Dimmesdale was afraid. "Who is that man, Hester?" he asked. "I am so afraid of him, he makes me shake! Do you know that man? I hate him, Hester!"

Hester remembered her promise. She did not say a word.

"Pastor," said Pearl, "I can tell you who he is!"

"Tell me quickly, then, child!" said the pastor. He put his ear close to her lips. "Quickly—and as quietly as you can!"

Pearl said something, but it was only silly words.

"Why do you make fun of me now?" said the pastor.

"You were not brave! You were not true!" said Pearl. "You would not promise to take my hand, and mother's hand, tomorrow at noon!"

Roger Chillingworth came up to Reverend Dimmesdale. "Good sir," he said. "Is it you? Come, my dear friend, and let me take you home."

Reverend Dimmesdale's voice was full of fear. "How did you know I was here?" he asked.

"To tell the truth, I did not know," said Roger Chillingworth. "I was with Governor Winthrop most of the night. I did what little I could for him. Now he has gone to a better world, and I was on my way home. I beg you, sir, come with me. Or it will be hard for you to do your Sunday sermon tomorrow."

The young pastor let himself be led away. His face looked cold and sad, as if he had wakened from an ugly dream.

5 Hester and the Doctor

It had been a strange meeting with Mr. Dimmesdale. The pastor seemed as weak and helpless as a child. Hester knew what his enemy was doing to him. She remembered the way the pastor had reached out to her that night on the scaffold. She remembered the fear in his eyes, and her whole soul was moved. Even though she had made a promise to Roger Chillingworth, she felt she had a right to help Mr. Dimmesdale.

For a long time, Hester had lived outside the laws and ways of others. She had no idea of right or wrong—only her own feelings. She was cut off from all other people but one. She and the pastor had done wrong together. And what they had done would hold them together forever.

At this time, people did not think about Hester the way they used to. Years had come and gone. Pearl was now seven years old. People saw her and her mother and the scarlet letter very often. Pearl and Hester did not seem strange anymore. The scarlet letter did not seem so bad.

For seven years Hester had lived quietly. She asked for very little. She only wished to share the same air as everyone else, and to make a living for herself and little Pearl.

When people fell sick, Hester was there, giving all the help she could. The scarlet letter was a mark of sin in other places. But in the sick room, it was like a candle. Hester did so much in times of trouble that many people gave her letter a new meaning. They said the A meant Able, because Hester Prynne was so strong.

She was a helper in the dark of night. When morning came, she was gone. Sometimes while walking on the street, she would meet someone she had helped. She never said a word. If the person tried to stop and talk to her, she put her finger on the scarlet letter, and walked on.

The scarlet letter had caused a great change in Hester. She had been beautiful. Now her beauty seemed burned away by the red-hot mark she wore. She seemed cold as stone. Her clothes were dull and dark. Her shiny hair was covered—hidden from the sun.

Hester's life had turned from her heart to her head. She had been an outcast for a long time. Now the laws of the day were nothing to her. In fact, some of her thoughts were crimes—worse crimes than the one that had earned her the scarlet letter.

Sometimes Hester's thoughts were very dark. It seemed too hard to bring up little Pearl. Everything seemed against Hester. The world was against her. Pearl herself had something wrong inside her. Sometimes Hester felt it might be better to send Pearl to heaven right away, and go there herself. Then God would judge her.

The scarlet letter had not done its work.

Now, after seeing Mr. Dimmesdale, she had something new to think about. She saw that the pastor was about to go crazy. His secret enemy had been at his side for a long time. And that enemy was hidden by the promise she made years ago.

Hester decided to see this man who had been her husband. She would do what she could to free Mr. Dimmesdale from him.

One afternoon she was walking with Pearl by the sea. She saw the old doctor. He was holding a basket and looking for roots and plants.

Hester told little Pearl to go down by the water, where she could play with shells and seaweed. The child flew away like a bird. Hester walked up to the old doctor.

"I must talk with you," said Hester. "It is something that is important to both of us."

"Aha! So it is Mistress Prynne who wants to talk to old Roger Chillingworth?" said the doctor. "With all my heart! Why, mistress, I have some good news for you! The magistrates have been talking about taking the scarlet letter off your dress!"

Hester said quietly, "If I were good enough, the letter would fall off by itself. Or it would be changed into something with a different meaning."

"Well, then, wear it, if that is how you feel," said the doctor. "It looks fine on your dress!"

All this time, Hester had been looking at the old man. She was surprised at the change in him. Before he had been calm and quiet. Now he looked almost wild. Sometimes she saw a red light in his eyes. It seemed as if his soul were on fire. In fact, old Roger Chillingworth was proof that if a man will do the devil's work, he can turn himself into a devil.

The doctor said, "You look at my face so carefully. What do you see in it?"

She said, "I see something that would make me cry, if there were any tears that were sad enough. But let it pass! I must talk to you about the pastor. You walk behind every step he takes. You look into his mind. You dig into his heart! You have a hold on his life. Every day you make him die a living death. And he still does not know who you are. Because I kept your secret, I have acted out a lie to him!"

"What choice did you have?" said Roger Chillingworth. "If I had pointed my finger at him, I could have sent him to prison. Perhaps I could have even sent him to his death."

"It would have been better if he had died!" said Hester.

"Yes, woman, you speak the truth!" said old Roger Chillingworth. The fire of his heart blazed out before her eyes. "It would have been better if he had died. No man has been hurt the way he has. He knew a hand was pulling at his heart. He knew an eye was looking into him. That eye was looking only for evil, and found it. But he never knew the eye and hand were mine. He thought he was being tortured by a fiend. And he was right! There was a fiend at his side. A man—who once had a human heart—has become a fiend just to torture him!"

Hester said, "Have you not tortured him enough? Have you not paid him back?"

"No—no! He owes me more!" said the doctor. "Do you remember me, the way I used to be, nine years ago? I know you thought I was cold. But was I not kind to other people? Was I not honest and fair?"

"You were all those things, and more," said Hester.

"And what am I now?" he said. "A fiend! Who made me this way?"

"It was I!" said Hester. "It was I! Why have you not taken revenge on me?"

Roger Chillingworth smiled. He put a finger on Hester's letter. "I have left you to the scarlet letter," he said. "Has that not given me revenge? If it has not, I can do no more."

"It has given you revenge," said Hester.

"I thought so," said the doctor. "And now, what do you wish from me?"

"I must tell the secret," said Hester. "He must know who you are. I do not know what will come of it, but this secret must be told."

"I feel sorry for you, Hester," said Roger Chillingworth. "If you had found a better love than mine, this evil would not have happened. I feel sorry for you, for the good that has been wasted in your heart!"

"And I feel sorry for you," said Hester. "For the hate that has made a good and wise man into a fiend. Why not forgive him, and be human again?"

"Peace, Hester," said the old man, in a hard, sad voice. "I could not forgive him if I wanted to. Since your first step into evil, everything has happened as it should. There is nothing we can do to stop this. Now go your way. You may do what you wish with that man."

He waved his hand and went back to looking for plants.

6 A Meeting in the Woods

As Roger Chillingworth walked away, Hester looked after him. She wondered if the young grass would turn brown under his feet. And where was he going? She wondered if all at once he would drop into the earth. And plants full of poison would grow up in his place.

Hester said, "Even if it is a sin, I hate the man!"

Hester told herself it was wrong to feel that way. But she could not stop herself. She wondered how she could have married him. She knew she had done great wrong to Roger Chillingworth. But it seemed he had done her an even greater wrong. For he had made her think she had been happy at his side.

"Yes, I hate him!" said Hester. "He did me wrong! He has done worse to me than I did to him!"

The old doctor walked out of sight. Hester called her child.

"Pearl! Little Pearl! Where are you?"

Pearl had been playing by the water. She had made little boats out of wood. She had put a jellyfish out in the warm sun to melt. When she saw some birds, she threw small rocks at them. Pearl was almost sure she had hit one little bird. It went away with a broken wing. But then Pearl was sorry. It made her sad to hurt something as wild as the sea wind. Or as wild as Pearl herself.

Then Pearl picked up some seaweed and made a letter A for her chest. "I wonder if Mother will ask me what it means," she thought.

Just then, she heard her mother's voice. She laughed and danced as she came up to Hester. She pointed her finger at the letter on her own chest.

At first, Hester said nothing. Then she said, "This green letter has no meaning on your little chest. But do you know why your mother wears a letter?"

"I do!" said Pearl. "It is for the same reason the pastor keeps his hand over his heart!"

Hester started to smile. But then her face turned white at Pearl's strange words. She said, "What does the letter have to do with any other person?"

"I have told you all I know," said Pearl. She was very serious. "But tell me, Mother. What does this scarlet letter mean? And why does the pastor keep his hand over his heart?"

"What shall I say?" thought Hester to herself. She was so alone in the world. She wanted to tell Pearl everything. But she told herself, "No! I cannot buy kind words from Pearl this way."

Out loud she said, "Silly Pearl. I like the letter because of its gold thread."

This was the first time Hester had not told the truth about the letter. All at once, Pearl was no longer serious. But she would not stop talking about the letter. Again and again, Pearl would look up at her mother and say, "Mother, what does the scarlet letter mean?"

The next morning, as soon as she woke up, Pearl said, "Mother!—Mother!—Why does the pastor keep his hand over his heart?"

"Quiet, child! Stop this talk, or I will shut you into the dark closet!" Hester had never said such sharp words to Pearl before.

Hester waited for a chance to tell Mr. Dimmesdale who his enemy was. She was afraid to go to his home. She knew Roger Chillingworth would be there. The only place that seemed right for a meeting with the pastor was under the open sky.

At last, Hester learned that Mr. Dimmesdale had gone to visit John Eliot, who was a missionary to the Indians. The pastor would be walking back to Boston the next day. So Hester took Pearl, as she always did, and went into the woods.

The day was cold and dark. There were gray clouds above. When the wind moved them, the sun made bright spots on the path.

"Mother," said little Pearl, "the sun does not love you. It runs away and hides. It is afraid of something on your dress. Now see! There it is, playing way over there. You stay here. I will run and catch it. I am only a child. It will not hide from me, for I wear nothing on my dress yet."

"And I hope you never will," said Hester.

"Why not, Mother?"asked Pearl.

"Run away, Pearl," said Hester, "and catch the sun! It will soon be gone."

Pearl ran off. Hester smiled, for Pearl really did catch the sunshine. She stood and laughed in the middle of it. Hester came up to Pearl.

Pearl shook her head. "The sun will go now," she said.

"See!" said Hester with a smile. "I can reach out my hand, and hold some if it."

Hester tried to hold the sunshine, but it went away. Pearl seemed to have pulled the sunshine inside her. It was strange how Pearl always seemed happy and in high spirits. But there was something hard about her. The troubles of other people never made her sad. She needed something to happen to her, something to touch her heart and make her care for others. But there was still time for little Pearl.

"Pearl," said Hester. "I hear someone coming down the path. I would like you to go and play, and let me speak with the man who is coming."

Pearl went away singing. Hester went down the path a little, where the trees made deep shadows.

She saw the pastor, leaning on a stick as he walked. He looked weak and sad.

At first she had no voice. Then, when Mr. Dimmesdale had almost gone by, she said, "Arthur Dimmesdale!"

"Who is it?" said the pastor. He looked at her. The shadows were so dark. Her clothes were dark, too. He wasn't sure she was real. He took a step toward her and saw the scarlet letter.

"Hester! Hester Prynne!" he said. "Is it you?"

"It is," she said.

They sat down. At first, they could only talk about the dark sky and the coming storm. Then the pastor set his eyes on Hester's.

"Hester," he said. "Have you found peace?"

She smiled sadly. She looked down at the letter on her dress. "Have you found peace?" she asked.

"None!" he said. "All my hope is gone. Hester, I am so unhappy!"

"People love you," said Hester. "And I am sure you do many good things for them. Does this not make you happy?"

"It makes me more unhappy! Only more unhappy!" said the pastor. "How can I lead them to heaven when my own soul is so evil? And as for people's love, I'd rather they hated me! I stand up in church in front of everyone. Their eyes look up at my face as if the light of heaven were shining there. Then I look inside myself and see what I really am. It makes Satan laugh!"

"You do yourself wrong," said Hester in a soft voice. "You have felt deeply sorry for what you have done. Your sin is behind you. And all the good you do for others—it must mean something."

"No, Hester, no!" said the pastor. "It means nothing. There is nothing in it. How happy you must be! You wear your scarlet letter on your dress where it can be seen. My letter burns in secret! If I only had one friend I could tell my secret! Or even an enemy!"

Hester Prynne looked into his face. She was afraid to speak. At last, she said, "You have that friend, and it is I." She stopped, and then she made herself go on. "And you have an enemy who knows your secret. He lives in your own house! That old man— the one people call Roger Chillingworth—he was my husband!"

The pastor sank down to the ground. He covered his face with his hands. "I might have known it," he said. "I did know it! In my heart, I was afraid of him. I hated him. Why did I not guess the truth? Oh, Hester Prynne! You do not know how awful this has been! How ugly for my sick and guilty heart to be open to this man! Woman, woman, this is because of you! I cannot forgive you!"

"You will forgive me!" said Hester. She threw herself on the fallen leaves beside him. "Let God punish me! You will forgive!"

She threw her arms around him. She pulled him close. She did not care that his cheek touched the scarlet letter. All the world had frowned on her for seven long years. And she had never turned away her eyes. Heaven had frowned on her, and she had not died. But she could not stand to have this weak, sad man frown at her. She could not stand it and live!

"Will you forgive me?" she said over and over again. "Will you forgive me?"

At last, the pastor said sadly, "I forgive you. May God forgive us both!"

7 A Plan to Go Away

They sat down, holding each other's hands. Above them, the trees blew in the wind. Neither of them wanted to go back to town. Here, in the eyes of Arthur Dimmesdale, Hester was not an outcast. And here, in Hester's eyes, Arthur Dimmesdale could be himself.

All at once, Arthur Dimmesdale said, "Hester! I have thought of something awful. Roger Chillingworth knows you planned to tell his secret. What will he do now?"

Hester said, "He is a strange man in some ways. He keeps things hidden. I do not think he will tell other people what he knows. He will look for another way to take his revenge."

Arthur Dimmesdale put his hand on his heart. "How can I live, living with my worst enemy? Think for me, Hester! You are strong! Choose for me!"

"You must not live with him any longer," said Hester. "Your heart must be free from his evil eye!"

The pastor said, "How can I be free? What choice do I have? Must I lie down on these fallen leaves and die?"

Hester's eyes filled with tears. She said, "You have become so weak!"

"Be strong for me," he said. "Tell me what to do."

Hester said, "You can be free from him. You can go back to England—to London, or Germany, France, or Italy. He could not find you there. You must begin a new life! You can be happy! You can do good work! You can trade your false life for a true one. Preach! Write! Act! Do anything—but do not lie down and die! Give up this name of Arthur Dimmesdale. Make yourself another. One you can wear without fear or shame. Get up, and go away!"

Arthur Dimmesdale said, "Oh, Hester! I am not strong enough or brave enough. I cannot go out into this strange, wide world alone!"

Hester said, "You will not go alone."

Then, they had said everything!

Hope and joy were in Arthur Dimmesdale's face. He also felt afraid. Hester was so bold. But he decided to go away—and not alone.

The reverend felt like a man who had been let out of prison. He said, "Oh, Hester! I had been ready to lie down on these fallen leaves and die. Now I can stand up again. I have new power to serve God. This is already the better life. Why did we not find it before?"

"Let us not look back," said Hester Prynne. "With this letter, the past is gone!"

She undid the pin that held the scarlet letter to her dress. Then she threw the letter away. It landed on the ground, near a little stream. Oh, how happy she felt! She took off her cap. Her rich, dark hair fell down around her face. She smiled. She was beautiful again. Suddenly, the sun made the dark forest bright.

Hester turned to Arthur Dimmesdale. She said, "Now you will know Pearl! Our little Pearl! She is a strange child. I do not really understand her. But you will love her, as I do. And you can tell me how to deal with her."

The pastor was fearful. "Do you think she will be glad to know me?" he said. "Children do not seem to trust me. I have even been afraid of little Pearl!"

"Ah, that was sad!" said Hester. "But she will love you. And you will love her. She is not far off. I will call her. Pearl! Pearl!"

While her mother was talking with the pastor, Pearl had been busy. She had picked berries. Then she had put flowers in her hair and on her dress. She heard her mother's voice and walked back slowly. She walked slowly because she saw the pastor.

Hester and the pastor watched Pearl as she walked up to them. Hester said, "Is she not beautiful? And I can see you in her."

Arthur Dimmesdale said, "I have been so afraid that other people might see myself in her. But she looks more like you!"

"No, no," said Hester. "She does not look most like me. Soon you will not be afraid to see how much she looks like you." She called again to Pearl. "Come, dear Pearl! How slow you are! Here is a friend of mine. He will be your friend, too."

The reverend saw Pearl looking at him. His hand went over his heart.

Pearl stopped walking and pointed her finger at her mother's chest.

Hester Prynne said, "Strange Pearl! Why do you not come to me?"

All at once, Pearl threw a fit. She waved her arms wildly and screamed.

Hester said to the pastor, "I see what is wrong. Pearl misses something that she has always seen me wear. I must wear it just a few more days. Then the sea will take it from my hand and keep it forever!"

With a sad face, Hester walked to the stream and picked up the letter. She put it back on her dress. Then she put her hair back under its cap.

"Do you know your mother now, Pearl?" said Hester.

"Yes!" said Pearl. "Now you are my mother. And I am your little Pearl!" She kissed her mother's cheeks. Then she kissed the scarlet letter, too.

"That was not kind," said Hester. "You show me a little love, and then you make fun of me!"

"Why is the pastor sitting there?" asked Pearl.

"He is waiting to see you," Hester answered. "He loves you, and your mother too."

"Does he love us?" asked Pearl. "Will he go back to town with us? Hand in hand?"

Hester said, "Not now, Pearl. "But soon he will walk hand in hand with us. We will have a home of our own. And he will set you on his knee and teach you many things."

"And will he always keep his hand over his heart?" Pearl asked.

Hester said, "Silly Pearl! What kind of question is that? Come over to him!"

But Pearl would not come to the pastor. Her mother had to pull her close to him. When the pastor gave her a kiss, Pearl ran to the stream and washed it off. She stood alone while her mother and the pastor talked, making their plans.

8 A Changed Man

The pastor left the forest ahead of Hester and Pearl. As he walked away, he looked back. There was Hester in her gray robe. And there was Pearl, dancing near the stream. So his meeting with them had not been a dream!

Mr. Dimmesdale thought of the plans he had made with Hester. They had decided to go to Europe. At this time, there was a ship in Boston's harbor, which had come from the Spanish Main. In four days, it was leaving for England. When the ship left Boston, he and Hester and Pearl would be on it.

Three days from now, the pastor was going to give the election sermon for the new governor. This was a great honor for any pastor. It would be a perfect way to end his stay in Boston. "At least," he thought, "people will have good feelings about me. No one will be able to say that I have not finished my work, or that I have done it badly."

The poor, weak pastor was lying to himself. No man can wear one face to himself, and another to the people. Soon he would not know which face is the true one.

The meeting with Hester had made the pastor feel strong. He walked back to Boston with a quick step. As he came into town, it seemed he had been away for many days or even years. Everything seemed to have changed. But it was the pastor who had changed.

The reverend met one of his deacons. He was an old man, wise and good. But when they talked, Mr. Dimmesdale could hardly stop himself from saying something wicked about the communion dinner. The pastor shook. He was so close to saying something terrible! But even though he was afraid, he wanted to laugh. How surprised the deacon would be if the pastor said such words!

Mr. Dimmesdale walked down the street in a hurry. He met an old woman. This woman had lost her husband, her children, and friends. But her love of God made her happy. Each time she met the pastor, he would tell her words from the Bible. But today the pastor could not think of any words from the Bible. He could only think of an argument that proved that when a person died, his or her soul would not live forever. If the pastor had told the old woman such a terrible thing she probably would have dropped down dead. What he finally did tell her, he did not remember. But she went away happy.

Next he saw a young woman. Her heart was clean and white as snow. Not long ago, she had decided to serve God. She walked up to the pastor. He knew that one word of evil from him would put a black spot on her heart. He covered his face and walked by without saying a word.

He saw a group of Puritan children playing. He felt like teaching them some very bad words. He saw a sailor who worked on a boat from the Spanish Main. He wanted to shake hands with the man, and trade jokes and curses with him!

The pastor walked more slowly. He thought, what is this? Am I mad? Do I belong to the devil?

Just then, old Mistress Hibbins, the so-called witch-lady, came up to him. She said, "So, reverend sir, you have been to the forest. Next time, let me know when you are going. I will be proud to come with you. I can promise you a good meeting with the ruler who lives there."

The pastor said, "I must say, madam. I have no idea what you are talking about. I did not go into the forest to see such a ruler. I only went to see the good Apostle Eliot."

"Ha, ha, ha," laughed the old witch-lady. "Well, we must not talk of such things during the day. You carry it off like an old hand! But in the dark night, in the forest, we will have another talk together!"

She walked on. The pastor said to himself, "People say the devil is that woman's master. Have I sold myself to him?"

The poor pastor. In order to follow a dream of happiness, he had chosen sin.

By this time, the pastor had reached his house. He went inside. There on his table was the election sermon he had been writing. He looked at the sermon. The man he used to be had written it.

There was a knock at the door. Roger Chillingworth came in. He said, "Welcome home, reverend sir. But dear sir, you do not look well. I think this travel in the forest has been too hard for you. Can I give you my help so that you will be strong enough to give your election sermon?"

"No, I think not," said the pastor. "The free air of the forest has done me good. I think I need no more of your drugs, though you give them in such a kind way."

The doctor looked at the pastor with a kind face. But Mr. Dimmesdale was sure the old man guessed that he had been with Hester Prynne. Soon, the doctor left.

That night, Mr. Dimmesdale threw his old election sermon into the fire. He began writing a new one. He wrote quickly, with deep and happy feelings. He was still writing when the morning sun came into his room.

9 A Holiday Sermon

Today was the great holiday. The new governor was going to take office. Hester and Pearl came into the marketplace. A crowd of people was already there.

Pearl wore a bright dress. She was in very high spirits. Sometimes she made loud, wild music with no words. Hester was dressed in gray. Her face was as cold and quiet as stone. But inside, her heart was as wild as Pearl's music. Soon she would be gone!

Pearl said, "See, Mother, how many strange faces. And Indians and sailors, too! Why have all these people come to the marketplace?"

Hester said, "They are waiting for the music and the soldiers. And then the governor and magistrates and the other great people will come."

In the crowd was the crew of the ship from the Spanish Main. Their faces were dark from the sun. They wore short pants and wide belts with buckles made from gold. They carried knives and swords.

The sailors did many things the Puritans could not do. They smoked and drank, right under the beadle's nose. No one punished them. The sailors followed their own laws. And the Puritans were not punished for being friendly to them. People saw Roger Chillingworth talking to the captain of the ship. But no one felt he had done anything wrong.

When the captain finished talking to Roger Chillingworth, he walked up to Hester. He said, "So, mistress, we will not have to worry about scurvy or fever on this trip! Now we have our own ship's doctor and this other doctor."

Hester said, "What do you mean? Someone else will be coming?"

The captain said, "Why, did you not know? This doctor here, Chillingworth, will be coming, too."

Just then, Hester saw Roger Chillingworth in the corner of the marketplace. He smiled at her.

Before Hester could think about what was happening, the music began. Slowly, the people playing music walked through the marketplace. Next came the soldiers, with their bright weapons and armor. The soldiers were followed by the governors and other officials. Last of all came Mr. Dimmesdale.

The pastor's step had never seemed so strong. His hand was not over his heart. But his strength did not come from his body. It seemed to come from his mind.

Hester looked at the pastor. All at once, she felt sad. The pastor seemed so far away from her. She thought of their meeting in the forest. How close they had been! Was this the same man?

Pearl said, "Mother, is this the same pastor who kissed me?"

Hester whispered, "Quiet, dear Pearl. We must not talk in the marketplace about things that happen in the forest."

Pearl said, "I was not sure it was he. He looked so strange."

Old Mistress Hibbins came through the crowd. People got out of her way. It seemed they were afraid to touch her. She walked up to Hester.

Mistress Hibbins said, "Who could believe it! That man over there seems to be so close to God. Who would believe that he has been in the forest?"

Hester Prynne said, "Madam, I am afraid I do not know what you are talking about."

The old woman shook her finger at Hester. "Ha!" she said. "I have been to the forest so many times! I know who else has been there! I know you, Hester. I can see your scarlet letter. You wear it where we all can see. But this pastor! The devil knows who belongs to him. Some people try to keep it a secret. But the devil has a way of bringing it out in the open, so that everyone can see. What is the pastor trying to hide, with his hand over his heart? Ha, Hester Prynne!"

The old woman walked away with a loud laugh.

By now, Mr. Dimmesdale had begun his sermon in the church. Hester could not make out his words, but she could hear his voice. It filled the air. It was sweet and very strong. The voice grew great and high. At the same time, it was like a cry—the cry of a heart full of guilt, asking God to forgive.

Hester stood next to the scaffold. She felt as if she could not move. Many people in the crowd were strangers. They had heard about Hester, but they had never seen her before. They came up to look at her and her scarlet letter. Hester felt as if the letter were burning into her.

Hester stood in shame at the marketplace. At the same time, everyone in the church was looking up at the pastor with eyes full of love. The great pastor in church! The woman of the scarlet letter in the marketplace! How could anyone think that the mark of shame was on both of them!

10 The Confession

The crowd came out of the church. The people were full of wonder at the pastor's sermon. They said a man had never spoken in such a wise and holy way. Their voices grew louder and louder until they became a shout.

All at once, the shout turned into a whisper. Mr. Dimmesdale was coming through the crowd. How weak he was! It seemed hard for him to walk. His face looked like the face of a dead man.

Old Mr. Wilson tried to help him. But Mr. Dimmesdale would not take his arm. He came to the spot where Hester and little Pearl were standing. He held out his arms.

"Hester," he said, "come here! Come, my little Pearl!"

Pearl ran up to him. She threw her arms around his knees. Hester also came—slowly.

Suddenly, Roger Chillingworth pushed through the crowd. He looked dark and evil. He took the pastor by the arm. "Stop!" he told the pastor. "What are you doing? Tell this woman to go away! And this child! Do not turn your good name black! I can still save you! Do not bring shame to yourself!"

Mr. Dimmesdale looked the old man in the eye. "Ha!" he said. "You are too late. Your power is gone! If God will help me, I can be free from you now!"

The pastor held out his hand to Hester. He said, "In the name of God, Hester Prynne, help me! Come, help me up to the scaffold!"

Hester helped him up. Pearl held one of his hands. Mr. Dimmesdale turned to the crowd. "People of New England!" he said. "You have loved me! You thought I was holy! Look at me here! I should have been here seven years ago! I should have stood up here with this woman! Look at her scarlet letter! You have turned away from her. But there was someone else you should have turned away from!"

The pastor stopped. He seemed too weak to go on. But then he stepped in front of Hester and Pearl.

He said, "There was someone else who wore a mark like Hester's! God's eye saw it! The angels pointed at it! The devil knew it well. But people could not see it. Until now. Now, before I die, I stand up before you. Look at what God does to people who turn against him! Look!"

He pulled away the clothes from his chest. The crowd looked at him in horror. The pastor stood, his face proud. Then he fell down on the scaffold.

Hester laid his head on her chest. Old Roger Chillingworth bent down beside him. "You have escaped me!" he said. "You have escaped me!"

"May God forgive you!" said the pastor. He turned to Pearl and said, "You would not kiss me in the forest. Will you kiss me now?"

Pearl kissed his lips. Her tears fell on her father's cheek. A spell was broken. What she had just seen made her a true person. She would not grow up wild and strange. She would not fight the world, but be a woman in it.

"Hester," said the pastor, "goodbye."

Hester put her face close to his. She said in a soft voice, "Will we see each other again? Can we be together after we both have died?"

"Hush, Hester, hush!" said the pastor. "God knows, and he is kind. God's will be done! Goodbye!"

That was the last thing the pastor said. The crowd broke out in a strange, deep voice of wonder.

People had different stories to tell about what they saw on the scaffold that day.

Most people said they saw a scarlet letter on the pastor's skin. They said the minister had tortured himself to make the letter.

Other people said Roger Chillingworth had made the letter with poison.

Some people said the pastor's guilt had made the letter.

And some said they had seen no letter on his chest at all. They also felt the pastor had said nothing about himself and Hester Prynne.

After Mr. Dimmesdale died, Roger Chillingworth changed. He was no longer strong. He seemed to dry up. He was like a weed pulled out of the dirt and left to lie in the sun. He had turned his life to revenge against the pastor. Now that the pastor was gone, his life was empty. He died before the year was over.

Roger Chillingworth gave a great deal of property to Pearl when he died. Pearl became rich. Soon after the old doctor died, Hester and Pearl left Boston. No one really knew what happened to them.

Years later, Hester came back to her small house. She came back alone. She still wore her scarlet letter. Often, letters came to her from another land. There were seals on the letters. The seals showed that Pearl had married someone great and noble. Once, someone saw Hester making clothes for a baby.

People thought that Pearl was married and happy. They thought that she would have liked to have her mother with her. But there was more life for Hester in Boston. This was the place where Hester had done wrong. And this was the place where she had been punished. She still punished herself. No one would have made her wear the letter anymore. She kept it on of her own free will.

People looked up to Hester now. They brought her their sad news and troubles. They asked her what to do. She helped them as best she could.

After many, many years, they dug Hester's grave. It was next to Arthur Dimmesdale's. There was one stone for both graves. And on that stone was a scarlet letter.